BROCKEN SPECTRE

BROCKEN

ALICE JAMES BOOKS
Farmington,, Maine
alicejamesbooks.org

SPECTRE

JACQUES J. RANCOURT

10 9 8 7 6 5 4 3 2 1

Alice James Books are published by Alice James Poetry Cooperative, Inc.,
an affiliate of the University of Maine at Farmington.

Alice James Books
114 Prescott Street
Farmington, ME 04938
www.alicejamesbooks.org

Library of Congress Cataloging-in-Publication Data

Names: Rancourt, Jacques J., author.
Title: Brocken spectre / Jacques J. Rancourt.
Description: Farmington, ME : Alice James Books, 2021
Identifiers: LCCN 2021007786 (print) | LCCN 2021007787 (ebook)
   ISBN 9781948579209 (paperback) | ISBN 9781948579445 (epub)
Subjects: LCGFT: Poetry.
Classification: LCC PS3618.A47995 B76 2021 (print) | LCC PS3618.A47995 (ebook)
   DDC 811/.6—dc23
LC record available at https://lccn.loc.gov/2021007786
LC ebook record available at https://lccn.loc.gov/2021007787

Alice James Books gratefully acknowledges support from individual donors, private
foundations, the University of Maine at Farmington, the National Endowment for the Arts,
the Amazon Literary Partnership, and the Maine Arts Commission, an independent state
agency supported by the National Endowment for the Arts.

 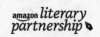

Cover art: Pacifico Silano, "You Shadow," 2019

CONTENTS

for Walter

When an observer stands on a hill which is partially enveloped in mist and in such a position that their shadow is thrown onto the mist, they may get the illusion that the shadow is a person seen dimly . . . that this person, or "spectre," is gigantic and at a considerable distance away from them.

—THE MET OFFICE, "Brocken Spectre"

NEAR THE SHEEP GATE

Many things
    I've reconsidered:
the snail's remarkable

    trail, the two slugs
slung around each
    other, organs

exposed & hanging
    from an outdoor
lamp. Because we live

    in the easier century,
today we say our
    wedding vows

& at night, when the heat
    drops, lunar
patterns, dark on dark,

    the cold stars break
like conversation.
    Had we been

born twenty years
        back, we might
be counted among

        the dead. Today I
promise to keep by your
        side, faithful as

night, if you dwindle
        into bedsheets.
In Jerusalem, near

        the Sheep Gate,
an angel of the Lord
        stirred a bathhouse

pool once a day
        which healed
the first submerged

        of whatever
disease he had. Child
        that I was,

I once believed
        faith to be a place
I lived inside myself

where the prayers
　for the sick did not
　　become prayers

for the dead. Where
　　they all could be
dipped to be cured,

　　transformed,
made new. Where
　　the pool was cool,

not warm; dark,
　　not incandescent;
thrashed & cut through

　　like a sash by
the man who stood
　　naked in the center.

A LIVING GIANT SQUID

My grandfather doesn't say much
about the war, except that it was
          his job to pull

the bodies, dead for three days
& rotting on shore, into sacks
          & stack them;

& that once when he yanked an arm,
the arm popped loose, tugged free
          from its torso,

leaving behind a socket;
& that the bodies reeked heavily
          like chocolate;

& that now, watching a show about
a research team, not far
          from Iwo Jima,

catching a living giant squid
for the first time
          on film by firing

a cloud of pulverized lesser
squid off the sub's bow,
        when the narrator says,

It doesn't take long for the dead
to summon the living, the narrator
        is wrong.

DISCOURSE ON THE METHOD

How I fed it, wad after wad,
toilet paper in the drizzling dark

the week I hiked into
the Hundred-Mile Wilderness

to become a man. It didn't take
(the fire, I mean), each offering

puffing up damply
in smoke, the roll growing thinner

& thinner & already (again)
the sharp need to shit. Fire

can introduce different colors & diverse
other qualities into different bodies,

but beside my body, my buddy
Chris watched me not make fire;

Chris, who I dragged along
on this spirit quest without thinking

that sharing a one-man tent might
look, on the outside, a little

like seduction; Chris, who wasn't gay,
but who wasn't not gay either,

when he had enough to drink,
but here, without beer,

was our dead-end. The markers we thought
we were following, the trail that

melts some bodies & hardens others,
consumes them almost completely,

the pines all stacked like fetches in a quiver
the night the mice drummed down

our sleeping bags *as admirable as anything*
that occurs in nature. Isn't this,

after all, what I wanted? To be miserable
& drenched with it? To come back,

transmuted from cinders into glass
& cut irrevocably, *solely by the violence*

of my actions? To not see, even for a moment,
who, or what, I wasn't? But this poem

is not about fire, *how it sometimes has heat*
without light & sometimes light,

but rather how the rain,
thickening, snuffed mine out

into scores of ashy scratches
& even these dissolved completely.

KIRBY

1990 LIFE *photographs by Therese Frare*

I have not forgotten
.his wrists
            stripped thin
his face set against

his father's face
hollowed
          fixed on
something outside

this room   Once I wanted
to be a martyr
             In this Ohio
pietà two nurses

swap out two bags
of saline
          a photographer
wipes clean her lens

with a cloth & through
a slit
         in the curtain
I can nearly see

his body failing
his spirit
              in equal measures
growing larger

as only someone
who did not live
                    through this
could possibly see

TRIPTYCH OF OUR FIRST DATE IN WHICH A MAN DIES FROM CARDIAC ARREST

1/

We walk through a park better known
       for its pleasures. At night the bushes barely conceal

what took place behind them—pants slumped,
       anchored down by belt buckles. Earlier, in our game

of searching the ground for spent condoms,
       we come across the baby rattler

sidewinding over the dirt & the ranger who tells us
       they're more venomous when they're young.

I want something timeless. I want you
       to tell me I could be more to you than just a body,

more than just what you could leave behind,
       though months will pass before I learn you do not

believe in the soul, that force that meant, I thought,
       we can make peace with the past so long

as its ghosts still inhabit a place, that meant we could blend

      into one another like the air that fills this park

from new leaves, bourgeoning with sex, or the hope for it,

      that fills my lungs when I take your hand while behind us

a man collapses

      just as you are about to speak.

When I recall what Lucretius wrote,

        that *Nothing comes from nothing,*

    I do not think anything

of the sapling sprung up from out

        the dead oak, nor do I wonder why

    these midnight cruisers

no longer lurk behind these trunks,

        cupping their crotches

    as if presenting a gift,

nor if their semen might thread still

        beneath us like roots,

    nor how a man's face could be transfigured

by the moonlight's shifting pattern

        through the old-growth groves,

    nor why the rangers thinned out this forest

one stalk at a time, nor how this parks sits

        where a tribe once lived

    before the Spanish king gifted the land

to the man who killed them. At the heart

              of every creation myth: *ex nihilo,*

     out of nothing, & though a universe

of zero size, one argument goes, comes as close

             to nothing as we can get,

     it is still not nothing.

In an emergency it's important,
I'll learn months later, to first establish

rank—*I'm a physician, I'm a nurse.*
Someone calls an ambulance,

someone offers you relief when
after five, ten minutes of pumping

his chest, the man's heart remains
still. Months later, you'll tell me

that in medical school they train you
to perform CPR to the rhythm

of the Bee Gees. Months later,
I'll confess that watching you

drive your weight so hard
that his ribs all snap, their snapping filling

the distance between us, that this
was when I first loved you. It's wrong,

I know, to fall in love
with someone while someone else is dying

in a park that's turned its face
to spring—or before, reaching out

to hold your hand just as his heart
halted & every remaining living thing

spurred into motion.

THE WAKE

what seemed necessarily bleak became.
two wet cormorants filling the branch of one tree.
more than just wading birds   more than just.
a lake   a dark scar at the center of my city.
more than anything I wanted to forget.
a time when desire named its price   in summer.
two hummingbirds take turns sucking one.
beardtongue dry   then I was born.
I say   in a place between two hills.
the year AZT was released   when I checked.
the records I was relieved.
that no one shared exactly my name.
that migration might mean the birds won't.
come back   that six hundred thirty-six.
thousand of us died & I did not.
know a single one.

HEAVEN'S KINGDOM

In my father's retelling
      of "The Talk," the stork—
            with a beak so big
he can barely walk—

wanders a beach in search
      of an oyster. He wants
            its pearl. But after he finds it,
after the oyster has finished

resisting, he cannot put it back.
      The moral?—patience
            in conquest, the price
of virginity. But rather than sex

I am thinking about the parable
      of the merchant who seeks
            the Kingdom of Heaven
& discovers it's a pearl

of great cost. Or the dream
      where my cousin comes back

                    from the beach
        where he killed himself, wet & smelling

of salt. The soul, like a pearl,
                is pale & baroque, but standing
                        here where he did it,
        where the gray waves swell & break

their heads against the rocks,
                the ocean's oysters
                        swarm against my feet
with their open, vacant mouths.

GOLDEN GATE PARK

Tonight, walking the AIDS
        memorial, I think about
the man who hydrated

        his partner by feeding
him ice chips with his
        mouth. Someone stumbles

down the path, maybe drunk,
        maybe a little
fucked up, & I know not to make

        eye contact, not to stop.
But I do stop. This man
        wants to fuck

right here & now
        on top of the red
earth. Back East where

        I grew up, the past persists
sinister as a forest: a man hit
        on another man

in a rural bar & thus
   was beaten with a cast-iron pan,
laid across the tracks,

   & severed by a train.
Here, his lips still sweet
   from the clove

he smoked, this stranger
   kisses me like those men
of our fathers' generation

   who'd rendezvous in parks
past dark. *Never again*
   will I destroy the earth

by flood, God told Noah
   after the sun broke
through, the covenant

   signed in rainbow.
Once, I believed in God.
   Convinced that the earth

was his own
   beating heart,
I talked to him out loud

       in the forest at night.
I felt endless then
         & knowing I wasn't

only enlarged me.

SAINT JOSEPH'S ORATORY

Montréal, Québec

Didn't I too once suck deeply from the bosom
of God? In a cathedral in a city that still succumbs

to the past, didn't I myself see two walls lined
with canes & crutches? & the pilgrims with crooked spines,

those who were paralyzed, were they not—at least some—
healed? & didn't I also leave with a great hum

like the St. Lawrence flooding the city gardens?
& how long after the last blast of the organ,

how long does that sound remain in the rafters
or against the dome's peeled plaster?

& when they exhumed the saints' corpses,
did they not still reek sweetly of roses?

& how far from the cathedral did the pilgrims walk
before they realized they still could not walk?

FRESHWATER EEL

I have seen our neighbor,
that old geezer, pull buckets
of them from under

his dock. Nocturnal, dark,
swathed by dorsal fins, their mouths
set in a kind of grin—to think,

how many times have I swum
this pond & nearly grazed
their skin? I do not swim again.

Many things remain
a mystery, but not this pond,
spring-fed & clear,

not its clouds of fish eggs
I break through on my way
to its center. At night

I lie belly-down on the dock
with my flashlight & wait
for one to appear

slithering under the surface
like Milton's Satan
halted by the sight of Eve

staring her own beauty
down in the pond's mirror.
For weeks now the Feds

have scoured the forest, acre
by acre, outside our house,
searching for an escaped

convict. At the outskirts,
the Cathedral Pines rise
a hundred feet up & what's left

below is dark & struggles
to grow. To think of him,
this man who raped & murdered

his own wife, a woman he must
have once found beautiful,
each night now lying on his back

on a pillow of moss & leaves
watching the meteors
flare through the breaks

in the branches.
Tonight, our neighbor
will wrap each eel in foil

with a sprig of dill, a slice
of lemon, & grill them on charcoal
& he will invite me over,

which I will decline
too enthusiastically, though
it should give me great pleasure

to take their pale rubbery flesh
into mine—these creatures
that live in clear water,

in the spring of beauty—
& to break their charred skin
with my teeth.

AT THE PLACE OF BATHHOUSES

[San Francisco]'s Public Health Director today ordered 14
bathhouses and sex clubs catering to homosexuals to close
immediately, saying they were 'fostering disease and death.'
—THE NEW YORK TIMES, *Oct 10, 1984*

A nondescript building with a nondescript name—

who would I have been back then?—where

the tile's grout, where the jizz drifting like smoke

through the Jacuzzi is holy. Thirty years since

& a man who lived on the other side of catastrophe

tells me he still prays for every man he fucked.

When lust's fog lifts, those who should have

showered, who smelled foul from it, those whose

cum shots lashed their faces & chests, those he let stay

inside him, all buttoned their shirts quickly. Always

I am the one leaving or the one who is left.

Nothing has ended; what happened before will happen

again—the fog belt will roll in with the chill

of the dead, the waves will cut the moon,

& I will watch from shore as the boys from seminary swim

naked in the sea. Or else I will be one of them,

at seventeen, buoyed by waves, hard in seawater,

those white Victorians dotting the hills.

IN FÁTIMA

1.

In Fátima in 1917, a woman in white *more brilliant than the sun* visited three children herding sheep.

2.

What she said in this vision (the voice firm & feminine, the Virgin Mary's) only confirmed what the children already deemed to be true—

3.

That they were special.

4.

& if they doubted what they saw (which they did not), they had only to kneel in the Portuguese field,

5.

Which had been wet but now was dry, which had been verdant but now was scorched,

6.

Or to look at the bodies of the cattle that lay struck down on the hill like bales of grain.

7.

Lúcia, the oldest, was nine

8.

& this woman who once gave birth to the son of God on her
side between two goats had asked her to spread a warning

9.

& she was too afraid to say no.

10.

The miracle seemed to be that the townspeople believed the
children,

11.

But in truth, they did not, not really,

12.

Despite the signs, despite the fact they believed that God did
live & could speak in mysterious ways.

13.

When their warning changed nothing & bombs still blud-
geoned craters toward Earth's heart,

14.

After the two younger children had died from influenza &
their cast-off bodies were buried sideways,

15.

When Lúcia had become an old woman, nearly a hundred
years old, after a whole history had passed her by,

16.

She began to doubt the visions, the fever-dreams she shared
in those afternoons of childish ecstasy,

17.

The nettle branches with which they had flailed their backs,
the boiling water with which they had scored their skin—

18.

Why hadn't the woman ever come back?

19.

Now Lúcia wonders if these memories are all merely shadows
of herself changing in the cloud patterns, like hands wringing
out a damp cold cloth.

20.

That God existed—she never doubted—

21.

But he watches over us from space like a meteor in orbit

22.

Or the large, sad eye of Jupiter.

23.

Truth be told even now she feels as important & alone as space

24.

Despite its stars, despite its occasional flares of violence.

PRELUDE TO THE NARROWS

Here change comes glacially   the Virgin River
     chiseling through   two thousand feet
& seven layers of limestone   over seven millennia
     where above the sun   razor-hot
cuts down   for a few minutes
     to where I stand   knee-deep in the runoff
unable to decide   if *decide* is even the right word
     what has ended   or begun

THE END HAS NOT YET PASSED OVER US

That God first placed an angel
        with a flaming sword to guard
    Eden's gates, that pleasure could poison,
      that he could punish us

even further—I knew. Yet when the Death Horse
        blazed through here, it did not stop
    for me, though I reached out a hand to course
      my fingers through its mane.

Snow falls. Termites eat out the tree's
        giant heart. I wish I could promise
    to remain unchanged had the plague passed
      through me. I wish the geranium

back to bloom, the frost back to the eaves,
        the fire back to the candles
    the children carried through the orchard
      the night it burned down. I want

the woman who flattens the snake with her foot
        to see how much blood it holds,

but what does this have to do with God?
I was careless, yes, & spared.

WHITE RIVER: AN ARGUMENT

      Each morning begins
with confession—
             That once I split

      open the lock-lipped
petals of a bearded iris
             to examine

      its spathe & haft.
That once I floated facedown
             underwater pretending

      to have drowned
& when no one noticed,
             I took off

      my bathing suit.
Oh, the trouble is
             water, a splake

      roughing the silt
with its tail-sail,
             carving law

into the sediment.
Oh, the trouble
            is erosion,

            the staircase I built
into a hillside, now
            seized up & rotted.

            If only I spent the day
on my knees forgiving
            the ground

            its give & rake,
its sharp intakes of breath.
            If only I pancaked

            my soul, flatfished,
against the river floor
            or became more like

            the hummingbird that
in one broad arc
            sucks a small bee

            down the needle
of its mouth—
            stinger & wings

      & all—
without the hesitation
           that comes

      with thought.
Therefore, in spring's
           black-soiled beauty,

      my head,
like Orpheus's, will be sad
           & hollow

      enough to float
toward sea by way
           of swift Hebrus.

AGAINST WHITMAN

I know that the decision to live doesn't come
from within, that even the smallest sprout shows
there really is no death.
                            Erosion leads us onward,
the cliffs that break us down, the sea that sweeps clean
our greatest triumphs, our mistakes—
the statue of a god
                            uncovered from seaweed,
the body of my cousin. All goes out & down
when everything collapses, but if to die
is different than anyone supposes—& *luckier*—
it begs the question
                            I have yet to ask.

A DETAIL FROM THE BAYEUX TAPESTRY, 11TH C.

Auspiciously the comet hangs
       in the tabby linen
above King Harold

the way the Hale-Bopp
       once in 1997
blipped over the funeral parlor

the night we buried
       my cousin
You'll never live to see this again

the aunties sighed the air thick
       with peepers
while thirty-nine of

Heaven's Gate Away Team
       attempted to reach
the spaceship trailing

the comet's wake
       that star-smear
across the sky no doubt

scrawling a sentence
       from some holy book
no doubt signaling

another turn toward war
       & further down
the tapestry ghost ships

cross a corrugated sea
       horses mid-gallop
trample the woven acres

between king & king—
       because all art once
was about conquest

history will remember
       those horses
even as time robs

the yarn of its dye
       even as I place
my hand to the glass

THE TOWN

It could've been worse,
      my mother says after
         lightning

struck down
      a white pine that
         took out

both our cars, the stump
      sharpened like
         a pencil,

It could've started a fire.
      True, her roads
         are dirt

& too narrow for crises.
      After fire, there'll be
         morels,

my mother says.
      After rain, spring
         flowers.

She believes in
    this shit:
        When God

closes a door. Above
    her toilet:
        Everything

for a reason. When I heard
    an acquaintance was no
        longer

engaged, I first
    thought they
        split

& when it became
    abundantly clear
        he died,

my hunger for gossip
    washed out. Yesterday
        I grew

angry at you over
    —what?
        spilled coffee?—

& imagined my life
     deliciously
         without you.

I'm sorry.
     East of here a storm
         struck

the Valley & started
     a grass fire. *Up until*
         yesterday

there'd been a town here,
     the woman on
         the radio

says, *& now there*
     isn't. Simple as
         that.

THE LOONS PROVE THAT EVEN BEFORE
THERE WAS A WORD FOR GRIEF
IT EXISTED AS SONG

Moreover when the orchestra's concerto
across the pond bounced off the mountain dome
& traveled to me across water

I knew that time & distance had changed the sound
the way music changes inside a prison chamber
which is why I've learned to listen

to the reverb pressing itself
into the spaces between where the body remains
but the spirit has forsaken

where the partridge sleeps in a mound of wet feathers
where the snake not at all evil stretches
in primal movements

across the damp sand
where the hornet struggles against a web
its green shell already partly eaten

where every word I whisper every begotten sentence
is a tombstone in a cemetery of teeth
where all night outside my window

I listen to the highway run like a river
that my cousin drives through back & forth
his hair growing thick past his ears then clipped

his life not lateral but horizontal
where the sound of his life
not passing by in years

is the same as the hornet struggling
against the web the same as
the spider's smallest mandibles

chewing through its head
because even a cell dividing in two is a sound
even thieves pillaging Cairo is a sound

even my cousin storing honey
on the sill of his bay windows
igniting the room into gold is a sound

that still exists somewhere in some echo
some mountain crater where he is moving away
into discordance where between us each year

this pond will freeze & thaw freeze & thaw
change forms change states
the salmon born down

under the vaulted ice the sunlight coming through
in arcs lit wicks cracks & fissures
which might look to the fish to be tunnels

to heaven if only fish were not
so dumb if only captivity were not the opposite
of heaven if only time were malleable if only

we could hold our breath for as long
as those loons that slip under our boat
in summer & resurface a mile away

into a place they did not choose

JUNE 12TH, 2016

The morning after the Pulse Nightclub massacre

Today when I go to Safeway
to buy lettuce, I discover I have
      no heart. You ask if I'm
all right after the shooting last
night & I tell you that
      I live

nowhere near Orlando. Dad let
out my cat to die today. He then calls
      to tell me that when she
had done dying her body leaked
a pool of clear liquid
      across

a patch of grass. The men last night
who danced openly in an open room,
      they jumped up & down in
a crowd like the bright mouths of koi
rising from the pond to
      swallow

whatever happens to fall in.
Today when I step on my shower mat
   I'm stepping on my cat.
Today this critter I loved more
than I love most people
     leaked out

a puddle like a bust faucet
& this was the fact that first broke me down.
   If there is just one thing
I should not grow accustomed to,
I am telling you now,
     I have.

THE BULLFROGS

Except for each note
        each slap-bass belch inflating
           their throats

        the bullfrogs sit on a half-
submerged log all damned day

           & stare me down
he-who-means-them-harm
        & do not flinch do not leap

for the pond water lapping
        their feet even when I creep closer
           in my kayak even when

        I'm only an arm's-length away
which may be why as a kid

        I so easily caught them
held their bulbous bodies
        with both hands to kiss

their broad squat lips
        which may be why
                I so rarely see them now

        though at night when I can't sleep
their humid chorus swells

                a cantor to what isn't dead
& by morning
        their singing ends

IN THE CASTRO

In these streets they marched, we march
from one club to the next,

bored of mojitos. Sometimes I look down at, say, the light
catching a crushed Coke bottle &, like that,

slip through to a time when all this meant
something different. I want to knock on each door

long before dawn until one of them
opens itself to me with fingers still caked

with wax. There are moments I get lost
in time, drawn low into that broken

glass throat, & then this place becomes
its very name: a buttress, *Castro,* these streets

where here alone we link pinkies
waiting for the bus & then in shop windows Polaroids

of strange purple cancers & then we're out
marching our candles down Market

& out marching our candles down
Market & out marching our candles—

oh, but I came too late.

NEAR THE END OF THE CENTURY

It's 1987, by which I mean
        I've been born,
     though barely, while in the heart
of Harlem strutters peck down
        a runway & speakers
     fray on about love:
park benches with no street lamps,
        examination rooms
     with no rubber bands
to bulge the veins blue. Time is elastic:
        either it's 1994, or it's 1980,
     or it was just last night,
it makes no difference: someone slips out
        the back screen porch
     of their parents' home
for the last time, someone leaves behind
        everything they know
     about how this will end
to the future to stand outside
        those warehouse doors,
     bass crushing their chest.
They might be a vision, then,
        if they could enter. They might

reapply mascara in the greased
bathroom mirror or duckwalk
            the runway, their hands
        two birds bickering above
their hair. They might make out
            with a ghost, they might
        twirl like a disco ball, spraying
every person in this room
            with flecks of lit glass
        until the host, clacking fans
with both hands, declares: *The old world*
            has passed away—
        Behold! All things have been
made new. But for now, it's not yet
            the end of the century,
        by which I mean
they have no reason
            not to believe her.

WESTERN WALL

I don't go to gay bars anymore
someone tells me & sure enough

another boards up   soon there won't be
a need for places like these

anymore   there's a word for what we lose
when we gain   our utopias

have all been urban have all been set
like jewels across the coasts we're from

different elsewheres   evenings I sat
with my father to watch the fish flick

the pond through dusk   I'll never go back
there is no queer pastoral

for a reason   I hold your hand
through public parks   the eucalyptus trees all

peel overhead into strips the koi
flutter through   we see another

queer couple making out on a bench
& some days it seems

we've found it   a holy city
swollen with light & sound

on the back of the tongue   so close
you could almost swallow it

I know it won't last   I've read
every myth   somewhere a western wall

still holds our prayers in its teeth
I want to be seen I want   to live

like in Jerusalem right before
or right after the siege

MT. DIABLO

California is burning & already the woods
where I first learned to love you

have withered, grayed. Last year
when fires rimmed the perimeter

of our city, we followed
in their wake, hiking

the underside of Mt. Diablo
& what was left by then already

blackened to polish, to mythic ash.
At dusk, our phones couldn't register

our city's distant lights,
so in the picture we stand smiling

before a black backdrop. A year ago
I barely knew you & now I picture

all the ways I could lose you—
what virions might already be

multiplying in your cells; what truck,
running an intersection, might barrel

over yours; what I might say
if I only had one sentence to say it.

Metaphor will be the first to go.
To walk through the moon's sea,

I told you on that hike, might look
like this—this burnt mountainside,

this Pompeiian aftermath,
lacquered to veneer. How here

we, like two astronauts, bob.
How here we, like two satans, patrol

the outer ring of hell's topography.
How I will love you through

prize & peril. Some Scheherazade
I've become, some Persephone,

telling you lies, yarn
after yarn, to keep you alive.

THE FALL

For Eve, choice
    didn't factor
when he offered

    her a fruit
so swollen it
    made her drunk

& after
    the first bite,
after the first

    sweetly cold
scent of fall,
    she ate it

core & all
    with the fever
of one

    who has never
eaten. To want
    is to live;

to refuse food
        is to admit
nothing more

        can be done.
In the club
        which is more

of a church,
        where the gobo
casts the floor

        into stained glass,
a younger man
        slips his hand

up my shirt
        to tug at
my nipple.

        Because
I want what
        anyone wants

who's watched
        the trees on
his street grow

       leafless & thin,
I take him back
       to my place

where he insists
       I go deeper,
snapping off

       my condom
without an edge
       of fear,

as if for him
       there is no
deep enough,

       as if for him
he never spoke
       his name into

a well's mouth
       to listen if
it came back.

JACQUES, FROM *JACOB*, RENAMED *ISRAEL*, WHICH MEANS, IN HEBREW, *HE WHO WRESTLES GOD*

Standing before it in Paris
in the fourth month of our long-distance

a morning after I had barely slept,
I could see what Delacroix meant

about his fresco, the one where Jacob
wrestles the angel, when he wrote

that it represents *torment*—
how he, like Jacob the night before

fording the Jabboq River, was alone—
whereas I might have argued

at a different time
that because of how Jacob's tunic is torn

down & off, how their fingers
in upraised hands interlock,

or how he leans his head against
another man's body, even the not-body

of an angel, that this fresco represents
the push-pull of sex—except

that pleasure is brief, it is fleeting,
so you could never

look at this painting & think
it had anything to do with sex,

or so I decided, standing before it in Paris
in the fourth month of our long-distance

the morning after I had slept
with somebody else.

GOLGOTHA

There is a home in every part of the world

A man tells another man this inside a tent that hides them

from everyone else   At the feet they become a multitude

When the ground shakes the man's frock rips

When the ground shakes a light seethes through the hill's maxilla

& it seems impossible to remain unchanged

to the man who asked for a man who would call out his name

MONSTER COCK

They're not allowed to be completely
nude, I recall in a deserted gay bar
when a go-go dancer, wearing

full camo, combat boots, a patrol hat,
inside a glass cube where a shower head
drenches him whole,

pulls out a cock roughly
the size of my forearm. This reminds me
of your patient, the homophobe,

who desperately needed a liver transplant
& got one when that night's winner
of the Big Dick Contest in the Castro

slipped off a barstool while getting
sucked off, hit his head against
concrete, & died. In this bar, the dancer

faces only me & the five-dollar bill
I cup & because the bar is empty
I avoid eye contact. It's one

of the unspoken rules, casting me
as Orpheus tunneling up the layers
of hell, as Lot's wife among the steel beams

corroded by salt. But because
I still, somehow, believe in the soul,
which transcends the body & triumphs

over death, which lingers over everything
like the cold dense fog that settles on
this city, I chance a glance

at his eyes under his hat's wide brim
through the shower's downpour,
even though I shouldn't,

even though he thumps
the heavy meat of his cock
against the glass.

WILD THOUGH THE SEA

Remember the night
    it snowed in a place

        we were told
    would never snow

& like two shadows
    cast by a lamp

        standing in the presence
of a Greater

we walked the beach
    the sand's grit refracted

        the expanse of what
I didn't know endlessly

swallowing the floes
    the ocean has always been

        immutable & dumb
has always carried on

past my limitations
      though they were many

          though I knew God
      the way I knew you

by being swallowed
      by giving my body over

          to the dead I am
      a creature after all

made am made
      to be touched

          through no fault
      of my own

WHERE TO BEGIN?

First: we were skinny-dipping,
Sam & I, in a pond in Tennessee,

which was his idea, I should say,
& the tree with the rope swing
loomed darker

than the dark night sky.

Second: the harvest moon,
which we were there for,

was nowhere to be found,
the sky instead burning with the stars
I couldn't see without my glasses

that Sam described for me.

Third: I've made no promises
to monogamy, but what to do
with those who have.

I spent my twenties riding
trains through cities leaving
behind hotel rooms

of men who may
or may not have been—

I never asked. The world of men
who have sex with men
is a chrysalis, a paper lantern

the hornets fill
with sound. Underwater, our feet
kept touching. *Sorry*, Sam said,

sorry, sorry, sorry.

I imagined his wife after
a bath, wrapping her hair
in a towel. I imagined

the cluster of small towns
I come from, each

with its own abandoned factory
with its own broken windows.

The world of men
who have sex with men
keeps to itself like the rock

hurled through the last
intact glass. *Shit happens,*
you know? Sam said

about fidelity as we stroked
from one shore

to the next. What we
did or didn't do

doesn't matter. He toweled off,
I treaded water, & the moon,
peering over the ridge

at last, silvered
the pond at its skirts.

AT THIS HOUR

In his car, an older man took me up
                              to see the city at night
& to run his bare hands over me.
                              Because as children
my cousin & I
                    deep-throated flashlights
to show each other
                              our skulls
while on the evening news
                         homosexuals unstitched
their skeletons, I'd been afraid
                                   of this
very moment. I understood
                              at seventeen,
better than anything about love,
                              that we must paw
over what we already know
                         to make it foreign again
in our hands. We live now
                         not then; T-cells dot
our veins, I told myself,
                         but when I kissed his throat,

I kissed in that column

                         a columbarium

for the dead men. Beyond his windshield,

                         the city-bruised sky,

each light another person

                         still awake at that hour,

still flushed

                         with blue breath.

AS WEATHER

Because at night the goldenrod & snake-grass
obscure the oncoming cars behind their gold,
the car seemed to bolt from *Nowhere*—

that place where tragedy is ripped from,
that place I'll visit at the very end of my life.
The car bolted from nowhere & rear-ended

mine, shoving it up & over & through
the guardrail into a cove of sapling eucalyptus.
Studies show just by walking through

a eucalyptus grove, under its strips
of peeling bark, its exposed stalks
the color of chicken bone, subjects reported

feeling noticeably happier, as if happiness
is a state you could enter through the gates
of its kingdom. My grandfather, for most

of his life, had a recurring dream of flying
over the Pacific, looking down at his shadow
crossing over waves & the dark mounds of whales.

He always woke before reaching his destination,
but he said, days before he died,
I feel like I'm getting close. There must be

someplace his terror goes. Or sorrow. Or love.
They must evaporate like sweat off skin
& return, eventually, as weather. All that remains

of fire after it burns down a forest: ashy smudges
tucked between the rings of trees, bruises
that never heal, screams pressed like petals

between the pages of history
where once I tried to write some lines
in an attempt to save my life

which, having done so, I could not forsake.

THE EARTH IS RUDE, SILENT, INCOMPREHENSIBLE

Now that we exist
     on the other
side of desire,

     when I tell you
I love you, I mean
     we live

on a planet
     that's dying
& it's no accident

     that the calla lily
is both the symbolic
     flower for weddings

& funerals. I told you
     that loons
mated for life

& when one died
the other spent
         her days calling

out to him across
         the gray pond.
Once again,

         you see,
I was wrong. Look,
         I will be

honest with you:
         when I promised
myself, I did so

         knowing not even
the sun lasts forever.
         Look! The future

is pressing itself
         so closely
against us it has already

         passed us by
& to die must make
         the same sound

as the woman
     I watched during
a rainstorm

     thrashing a river
with a branch.
     Could we make

time pass
     a little more
slowly? I want

     to watch
the fireflies spark
     up the tallgrass

& the bullfrog,
     that unrolls
its wide fat tongue

     a thousand
frames per second,
     thwap the fly

that flickers
     before it
with its honey-thick spit.

VOYEUR

Whatever I expected,
    it was not that the dungeon
would be stone-quiet, that the men
    pacing the halls for sex would be
polite. They, like me, came out *after,*
    while in the center pool, the old
men soak. These tunnels, dark & damp,
    industrial steel halls that snake,
offer doors with slots for passersby
    to watch where, inside, men wait.

I wanted to see if the bathhouse
    would permit me. If walking
this labyrinth would be like walking
    into the past. Or like when a storm
rolled in over the hills, how I watched
    from underwater for rain
to break the river's ceiling. The men
    in the pool, the ones who remember,
they lift themselves in & out.
    They are like a council of stars

lit blue from underneath. They laugh
    silently & touch each other,
or float on their backs, staring up
    at the show of light on the ceiling.
They lean their heads against
    each other as water drips in pearls
from their soft arms, half
    in this world, half in another.
& for a long time, from behind
    the grill's steel grate, I watch them.

LOVE IN THE TIME OF PrEP

To see more clearly, we climb
            the shifting sands
                        of Haleakala volcano.
The guidebook says we might be haunted
            if the mist & the light

are just right & sure enough,
            a rainbow haloes my head's
                        shadow. *Brocken spectre*
it's called & *Isn't this awesome,*
            you, my dorky husband, say.

You are thinking about science again,
            about how light & water particles
                        bounce & interact & refract
against each other, whereas I,
            the melodramatic poet, see

some paranormal visitor,
            some queer saint. Back home in bed
                        you tell me how in the early '90s to you
coming out meant either you killed yourself
            or you died from AIDS

& you chose to come out anyway.
        Time moves like bluffs,
                like erosion. It flattens
to rift & split. It carves down
        the precipice like the runoff

we clambered up to find
        the path already deteriorated.
                I hiked in just flip-flops
& when a thong broke
        I hiked in bare feet.

Let's go back some day. Let's go back
        to where the ocean's panorama
                was endless & shimmering,
where the violets bursting forth
        were reminders that the world

will go on generously without us.
        In bed, I kiss you between
                your shoulder blades & say,
I'm glad you're here. North of us,
        two freshmen are skipping class.

They are learning. They are taking turns
        taking each other raw,
                as if they alone are discovering

something new. As if none of this
ever happened.

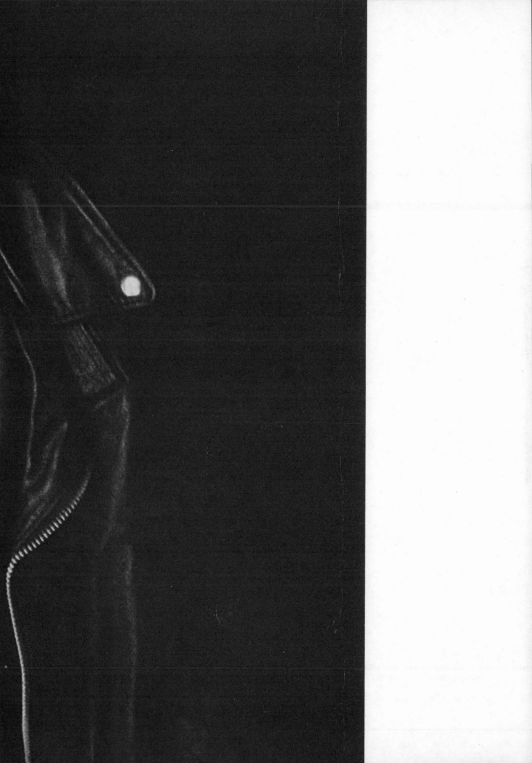

NOTES

"Near the Sheep Gate": John 5:1–4.

"A Living Giant Squid:" The italicized line is adapted from the commentary of the Discovery Channel's show *Curiosity,* "Monster Squid: The Giant Is Real."

"Discourse on the Method": The italicized lines are lifted and modified from Descartes' *Discourse on the Method* (1637) translated by Paul J. Olscamp. This poem is for CCC.

"The Wake": The statistic of 636,000 lives lost in the United States to complications of HIV/AIDS since the epidemic began comes from the Centers for Disease Control and Prevention (CDC) in 2014, the year this poem was written.

"Heaven's Kingdom": This poem is for my father and for Russell Jr.

"Against Whitman": Section VI of Walt Whitman's "Song of Myself."

"In Fátima": The quoted line comes from an account by Sister Lúcia de Jesus Rosa dos Santos.

"Triptych of Our First Date in Which a Man Dies from Cardiac Arrest":

The argument in the second section refers to Alexander Vilenkin's definition of nothing.

"A Detail from the Bayeux Tapestry, 11th C.": "By far the most famous appearance of Halley's comet occurred in 1066, when it coincided with the Norman Conquest . . . later included in a section of the famed Bayeux Tapestry, which depicts King Harold and a crowd of fearful Englishmen watching it streak through the sky" (History.com). And: "Those who designed the Bayeux Tapestry were obviously horse lovers . . . the different gaits can be observed in the horses actively engaged in combat. Some rush headlong at the enemy, some are struck by the Housecarls' axes, some are rearing up and others collapse" (Bayeux Museum). Lastly, this poem also makes reference to the members of the Heaven's Gate religious cult which participated in a mass suicide between March 22nd and 26th, 1997, by consuming phenobarbital mixed with applesauce.

"In the Castro": This poem owes a debt to David Weissman's documentary *We Were Here.*

"*Jacques*, from *Jacob*, Renamed *Israel*, which Means, in Hebrew, *He Who Wrestles God*": "Throughout his life, Delacroix engaged in the artist's solitary struggle, constantly measuring and challenging his own creative powers, and—why not?—pitting himself against God the Creator, in the person of the Angel. Like Jacob on the night before crossing the ford over the Jabboq river, he is alone" (Musée National Eugène Delacroix).

"The Fall": The line "There's no deep enough" is lifted and modified from Jorie Graham's poem "The Age of Reason."

"Near the End of the Century": The italicized lines quote 2 Corinthians 5:17. Additionally, this poem was sparked by Randall Mann's "The Fall of 1992" and John Murillo's "Dolores, Maybe."

"Wild Though the Sea": The title comes from a line in Emily Dickinson's poem, "How sick—to wait—in any place—but thine."

"The Earth is Rude, Silent, Incomprehensible": The title comes from section IX of Walt Whitman's "Song of the Open Road." This poem is for Walter, written the morning before our wedding.

"Love in the Time of PrEP": PrEP (pre-exposure prophylaxis) is a pill taken daily to reduce the risk of contracting HIV. The lines "In bed I kiss you / between your shoulder blades & say, / *I'm glad you're here*" are lifted and modified from Chuck Carlise's poem, "A Hole of Bones & Thread."

ACKNOWLEDGMENTS

Grateful acknowledgment to the editors of these journals where the following poems first appeared, sometimes in alternate versions or with different titles:

32 Poems: "Saint Joseph's Oratory"

The Adroit Journal: "Western Wall" and "Heaven's Kingdom"

The Baffler: "Where to Begin?"

Beloit Poetry Journal: "At the Place of Bathhouses," "Kirby," and "The Wake"

Boston Review: "Jacques, from Jacob, Renamed Israel, Which Means, in Hebrew, He Who Wrestles God."

The Cincinnati Review: "A Detail from the Bayeux Tapestry, 11th C." and "The Town"

Colorado Review: "Voyeur"

Copper Nickel: "Freshwater Eel" and "Monster Cock"

Foglifter: "Triptych of Our First Date in Which a Man Dies from Cardiac Arrest" and "The Bullfrogs"

The Georgia Review: "Love in the Time of PrEP"

Gulf Coast: "Near the End of the Century"

The Journal: "Golden Gate Park" and "Near the Sheep Gate"

Kenyon Review: "Against Whitman" and "Golgotha"

Memorious: "In the Castro"

Missouri Review: "Discourse on the Method"

Nimbus: "Prelude to the Narrows"

Ninth Letter: "The Fall"

Ploughshares: "Wild Though the Sea"

Poetry Northwest: "Mt. Diablo"

Prairie Schooner: "In Fátima," "June 12th, 2016," and "The Loons Prove
   That Even before There Was a Word for Grief It Existed as Song"

The Rumpus: "As Weather"

Southern Indiana Review: "A Living Giant Squid" and "The Earth Is
   Rude, Silent, Incomprehensible"

Spoon River Poetry Review: "White River: An Argument"

Virginia Quarterly Review: "The End Has Not Yet Passed over Us"

Many of these poems appeared in the chapbook *In the Time of PrEP,* published
by the *Beloit Poetry Journal* (2018). "A Living Giant Squid" was reprinted
on *Poetry Daily.* "Against Whitman" was republished in *Be Wilder: A Word
Portland Anthology.* "The Earth Is Rude, Silent, Incomprehensible" was
reprinted in the *ALL Review.*

My love and appreciation to Molly Bashaw, Eavan Boland, Melissa Crowe,
Joseph Fasano, Richie Hofmann, Jessica Jacobs, Josh Kalscheur, Christopher
Kempf, Chaney Kwak, Corey Van Landingham, Rosalie Moffett, D. A. Powell,
Laura Romeyn, Casey Thayer, Jim Whiteside, and Shelley Wong for their
invaluable feedback and insights on this book.

To Carey Salerno, Alyssa Neptune, Julia Bouwsma, and everyone at Alice
James Books: thank you.

My gratitude to all my teachers and mentors whose guidance have shaped
me. My thanks to Stanford University's Wallace Stegner program where I

wrote some of these earliest poems, to the Cité Internationale des Arts where this manuscript first found its voice, to the Bread Loaf and Sewanee Writers' Conferences for the community.

And to Walter, whose love and faith in me has never faltered.

RECENT TITLES FROM ALICE JAMES BOOKS

ALICE JAMES BOOKS is committed to publishing books that matter. The press was founded in 1973 in Boston, Massachusetts as a cooperative, wherein authors performed the day-to-day undertakings of the press. This element remains present today, as authors who publish with the press are invited to collaborate closely in the publication process of their work. AJB remains committed to its founders' original feminist mission, while expanding upon the scope to include all voices and poets who might otherwise go unheard. In keeping with its efforts to build equity and increase inclusivity in publishing and the literary arts, AJB seeks out poets whose writing possesses the range, depth, and ability to cultivate empathy in our world and to dynamically push against silence. The press was named for Alice James, sister to William and Henry, whose extraordinary gift for writing went unrecognized during her lifetime.

Designed by Alban Fischer
Printed by McNaughton & Gunn